TRUE
CRIME

Cyber Crime

John Townsend

Raintree

Chicago, Illinois

For information, address the publisher:
Raintree, 100 N. LaSalle, Suite 1200, Chicago, IL 60602

Customer Service: 888-363-4266
Visit our website at www.raintreelibrary.com

Printed and bound in China by South China Printing Company.
08 07 06 05 04
10 9 8 7 6 5 4 3 2 1

Library of Congress Cataloging-in-Publication Data
Townsend, John, 1955-
   Cyber crime / John Townsend.
     p. cm. -- (True crime)
   Includes bibliographical references and index.
   ISBN 1-4109-1093-8 (library binding) -- ISBN 1-4109-1170-5(pbk.)
    1. Computer crimes--Juvenile literature. 2. Cyberterrorism--Juvenile
literature.   I. Title.
   II. Series: Townsend, John, 1955- . True crime.
   HV6773.T68 2004
   364.16'8--dc22

2004012876

Acknowledgments
Alamy pp. 13, 34, 19 (Don Tremain), 22 (Image source), 11 (Mike Hill), 8 (National Motor Museum); Associated Press pp. 9, 18, 38–39, 16 (Canadian Press/Andre Forget); Corbis pp. 20, 32, 36–37 (Bill Stormont), 35 (Charles O'Rear), 29 (Chris Hardy/San Francisco Chronicle), 38 (Gregory Pace), 22–23, 25, 30, 42, (Harcourt Education Ltd), 27 (Jose Fuste Raga), 37 (Leif Skoogfors), 10–11 (Pete Saloutos); Corbis Sygma pp. 14–15 (Gordon Chet), 9 (J Bounds-RNO); PA Photos p. 34; Photodisc/ Harcourt Education Ltd pp. 4–5, 5, 14, 16–17, 21, 32–33, 41, 43; Ronald Grant archive pp. 6–7; Science Photo Library pp. 12 (Andrew Syred), 33 (BSIP Laurent/H Amerciain), 7 (Jerry Mason), 42–43 (Martin Dohrn), 12–13 (Victor Habbrok Visuals); The Kobal Collection pp. 6, 24, 32–33 (Mayfair/Transcas), 30–31 Paramount/Gordon, Melinda Sue); Tudor Photography pp. 28, 40–41.

Cover photograph of man at computer reproduced with permission of Corbis/Hermann/Starke.

Every effort has been made to contact copyright holders of any material reproduced in this book. Any omissions will be rectified in subsequent printings if notice is given to the publishers.

The paper used to print this book comes from sustainable resources.

Contents

Any words appearing in the text in **bold** are explained in the glossary. You can also look out for them in the "Word Bank" at the bottom of each page.

What is a cyber crime?

- Accessing a computer without permission.
- Stealing information from a computer.
- Sending data that damages a computer system.
- Accessing or sending secret or illegal information.

Whether a door is open, closed, or locked, a thief will try to get inside. That may mean:
- stepping through an open doorway;
- turning the handle and pushing it open;
- breaking the lock before barging right in.

All three are against the law if the room inside is private. This crime is called breaking and entering, even if nothing is stolen.

It is just the same with computers. Gaining **access** to someone's computer is a crime. Cyber crime is anything **illegal** to do with computers. Causing harm or stealing through computers is serious cyber crime that now carries a heavy **penalty.** It is also big business.

accessing   getting inside
data   information stored on computers

Cyber criminal

What does a criminal look like? Someone in a mask with a gun? A figure creeping around at night? A teenager sitting at a computer with a cup of coffee in a cozy bedroom?

Believe it or not, they could all be bank robbers. But the last one, the cyber criminal, does not need to leave home. All he or she needs is a computer. There are no alarms and no car chases. It is all done with a click of the mouse and a few taps on a keyboard. The wires that link up the **World Wide Web** carry billions of bits of **data** around the globe each second. All ready for attack.

Find out later...

What harm can cyber **vandals** do?

What do cyber thieves steal?

What are cyber terrorists?

penalty   punishment for breaking the law
vandal   person who sets out to destroy or damage someone else's property

Sneakers

In 1981 Captain Zap was the first person to be **convicted** of a computer crime. He broke into a U.S. telephone company's computers and changed the timing system. This let him make cheap phone calls during peak hours. He later hacked into military computers and was sent to prison. The 1992 movie *Sneakers*, below, was based on some of his crimes.

Very few people owned computers 25 years ago. More people began using them in the 1980s. A few years later, the world entered the **Internet** Age. But cyber crime was already under way.

Even in the 1970s, thieves known as phone phreakers in the United States figured out how to **access** the telephone **network.** They could then make free calls all around the world. This was the beginning of electronic crime. In 1972 a man known as Captain Crunch was caught making free long distance calls. He was sent to prison for **fraud.** Now he runs a computer security company to help protect people from cyber crime.

Word Bank

fraud   false or dishonest trick to get money
military   armed forces of a country

The new world

In 1981 the computer company IBM came up with a new type of machine. It was a **stand-alone** machine called a personal computer (PC). PCs were soon used in many offices for storing **data.** Then something big happened. Computers were linked up to "talk" to other computers across ordinary phone lines.

In 1983 the Internet was first started for universities and the **military.** In the same year, a movie came out that gave a chilling warning about this new computer world. *Wargames* was about a teenager who broke into a military computer system. He almost caused a world war by mistake. The film showed a scary new world.

Code names

Hacker: Someone who uses his or her computer skills to break security for a challenge.

Cracker: Someone who often gains access to computer systems to steal.

Sneaker: Someone hired to break into computers to test their security.

In the movie *Wargames*, Matthew Broderick plays a teenager who **hacks** into the government's defense system.

stand alone   computer that is not linked up to any other computer

In 1990 Kevin Poulsen was arrested after hacking into all the phone lines going into a Los Angeles radio station.

The station was giving prizes to the 102nd caller that day. Poulsen made sure it was him. He won a Porsche like the one above. But his luck ran out. The **FBI** caught up with him, and he went to prison for **fraud**.

Growing fast

By the mid 1990s, the **Internet** had over sixteen million **websites** and was growing fast. This world-wide computer **network** linked up many smaller networks to make a huge web of links. This became known as the **World Wide Web** (WWW). Information was now speeding around the world as never before. Banks began to deal with huge amounts of money through the Internet.

In 1994 Russian hackers broke into the computers of Citibank. They took more than $10 million. The ringleader, Vladimir Levin, was arrested in London a year later. Citibank got most of the stolen money back.

Crime wave

Kevin Mitnick was seventeen when he first began **hacking**. In 1989 he went to prison for stealing **software**. When he was released, he started hacking into computers of **credit card** companies. He stole 20,000 credit card numbers. Once more he was sent to prison for five years. In 2000 he was released from prison. Even though he had caused millions of dollars of damage, he said he had not meant to cause harm.

FBI   Federal Bureau of Investigation, which deals with serious crime in the United States

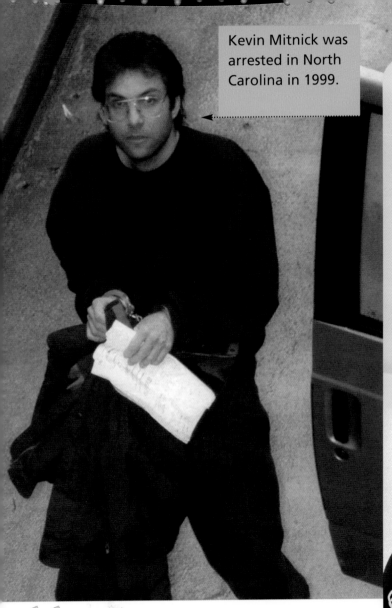

Kevin Mitnick was arrested in North Carolina in 1999.

Behind bars

In 1994 Kevin Poulsen (below) was sentenced to four years in prison for cyber crimes. He also had to pay $56,000. It was the longest sentence ever given for hacking. Kevin later pleaded guilty to breaking into FBI computers. He now writes about computer security.

BK
29384 09·08·90
LOS ANGELES POLICE= JAIL-J

> I am not innocent, but I didn't do most of what I was accused of. I never made any money directly from hacking.
>
> Kevin Mitnick, 2001

software   systems that run computers and allow them to do different tasks

making trouble

Millennium bug

At midnight on December 31, 1999, the world held its breath. Many people feared all computers would **crash** at the start of the year 2000—the new **millennium.** They thought the date change would close down **networks.** Hackers could then do great damage. Would the **Internet** be lost forever? Would banks lose a fortune? It was a tense time. But nothing happened!

Like any house, a computer can be made fairly **secure.** But if thieves are determined to get inside, they will find a way to break in. And once they are inside, they may:

- steal money to keep for themselves;
- steal goods to sell to others;
- go around and wreck every room.

Some cyber criminals do just that. They enjoy wrecking someone else's computer system. Often they simply want to show off by saying, "I know how to cause damage. I've got power. Think about what I could have done." Cyber **vandals** get a thrill from harming the work of others. They can also do much worse.

Graffiti is a form of **vandalism.** It is ruining someone else's property, just as cyber vandals do.

Word Bank   boot sector   program that loads a computer's operating system

Harmless fun?

Is there any harm in **hacking** into a **website** to change it slightly? Some cyber criminals think this is just fun. But what if important information is changed to mislead or upset people?

Some vandals write **software programs** that spread and damage computer systems. These programs are called **viruses.** The results are far from fun. Health and emergency services depend on computers. Cyber vandals could harm lives if they disrupt these services.

Some people think cyber criminals are heroes who "beat the system." They think it is brave to bring rich and powerful organizations to a halt. But innocent people often become the victims.

Tricks

Virus writers have learned new tricks. One is to load viruses into a computer's memory so that it keeps running while the computer stays switched on. Another trick is to infect the **boot sector** on floppy disks and **hard disks.** This makes sure the virus gets into the computer's memory right away.

Cyber vandals put people's lives at risk.

hard disk   main storage space and memory on a computer
secure   safe against attack

Worming into the system

Worms are viruses that spread quickly. They are designed to keep making new copies of themselves. A worm might just get into a computer and leave a silly message—or it might destroy the **hard disk**.

The worm

Some cyber **vandals** try to **infect** the **software** that computers use. They have developed a special kind of **virus** called a **worm** to do this. When it gets inside a new machine, it starts to make lots of copies of itself. The worms keep multiplying as they get sent over the **network**.

Some worms go into a computer's address book. They get sent as emails to all the stored addresses—without the user's permission. If many computers do this at the same time, the **Internet** becomes overloaded and will **crash**.

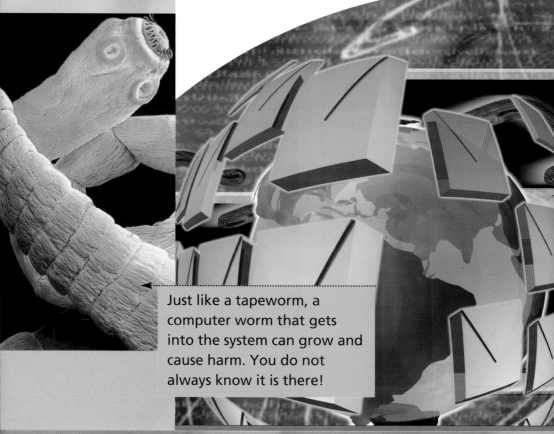

Just like a tapeworm, a computer worm that gets into the system can grow and cause harm. You do not always know it is there!

infect   pass on something harmful to someone else

An expensive mistake

One of the first worms to hit the Internet began as a **program** that went wrong. Robert Morris was a college student who was learning about computer science. He created a program that got into the Internet in 1988. The Internet Worm crashed 6,000 computers, including a **NASA** network. In 1990 Morris was sentenced to three years **probation.** He had to pay a fine of $10,000.

Morris was one of the first people to be **convicted** under the U.S. Computer **Fraud** and **Abuse** Act. He must have learned a lot from his mistake, because today Morris is a computer professor.

Did you know?

Another type of cyber **vandalism** uses a Trojan horse. This is a program that looks like a game or a good piece of software. When you **download** it and run it, it wipes out your hard disk, and your computer becomes useless.

According to an ancient story, the Greeks won the Trojan War by hiding in a huge hollow wooden horse. They used this to sneak into the guarded city of Troy and attack.

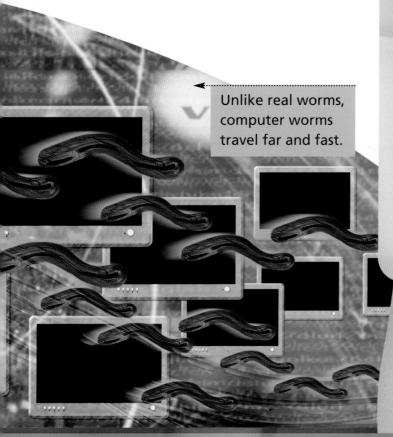

Unlike real worms, computer worms travel far and fast.

The hoax

Most comuter **hoaxes** turn out to be harmless. But some cost a huge amount of money and cause a lot of stress.

One of the most famous hoaxes to hit computers in 1994 was called Good Times. An email warned people not to open messages with "Good Times" as the subject. It said that a virus would wipe out their computer's entire memory and that they should warn others. Frightened users sent warnings to everyone in their address book. Many **servers crashed** under the strain, which stopped them from working.

To...	Kate
Cc...	
Subject:	EMAIL VIRUS

Do NOT open emails with "Good Times" in the subject header

Hi,

Please make sure you do not open emails with "Good Times" in the subject line, since these contain a virus.

This virus will wipe out your computer's memory. Please forward this warning to everyone you know.

Thank you

hoax   practical joke
icon   image or sign on a computer screen

Red Alert

In 1996 computer users began to panic when they got an email alert that warned them not to visit the **Microsoft website.** If they did, their computer would catch a **virus** that would wipe it clean and make it useless. It was called the Red Alert Virus. But the whole thing turned out to be a hoax.

Like a lot of computer hoaxes, it ended with: "Please pass this message on to as many people as you can." This is how a lot of hoaxes keep going. Another twist of this hoax came in November 1999. It just said:

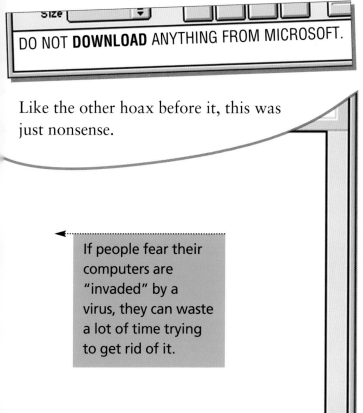

DO NOT **DOWNLOAD** ANYTHING FROM MICROSOFT.

Like the other hoax before it, this was just nonsense.

If people fear their computers are "invaded" by a virus, they can waste a lot of time trying to get rid of it.

Watch the teddy bear

In 2002 many people were fooled by an email. It told users to **delete** the file Jdbgmgr.exe because it was a harmful virus.

This file has a teddy bear **icon** (below). In fact, the file is an important system file for running the Windows **software.** Without it, computers will not work correctly.

Big trouble

In 2000 a seventeen-year-old Canadian boy (code name Mafia Boy) was found guilty of attacking **websites**. He made over fifty computer attacks, including the ebay Amazon, Yahoo, and CNN websites. He was lucky. He was sentenced to only eight months in jail and fined $250. Most computer vandals face much tougher sentences.

Cyber **vandals** get a thrill from seeing things go wrong. But some like to show off about it, and this is how they end up getting caught. Their bragging often gives them away.

There are two sorts of cyber vandal:
- cyber punks: they are usually between 12 and 30 years old. They have grown up with computers and learned their skills early. They often brag **online** about **hacking** into systems to **vandalize** them. Often they do not realize what harm they cause.
- coders and **virus** writers: these people have a lot of programming knowledge and can write viruses that quickly spread across the **Internet**. Coders usually know what damage they will cause.

Mafia Boy arrives at court in Montreal, Canada—unable to show his face.

Word Bank   anti-virus software   software that tracks down a computer virus and makes it safe

Spreading like fire

Like some human viruses, a computer virus spreads quickly. Viruses attached to emails can pass around the world in minutes.

Sometimes the computer user has no idea a virus has struck. Sometimes a message appears on the screen on a set date. That might be all it does. Others are far more harmful and are designed to wipe out files.

Viruses can soon clog parts of the Internet, since millions of messages flood into a **server** at once. **Anti-virus software** is now big business. Internet users can **download** "patches" or **programs** to protect their machines. They are trying to keep one step ahead of the vandals.

Real viruses can grow and spread fast.

The work of the cyber vandals

Virus writers have tried hard to cause **chaos** over the last twenty years. In 1989 only about 30 viruses appeared. Two years later, there were more than a thousand going around the **Internet**.

Vandals release new viruses every day. One of the first viruses to **infect** computers struck in 1987. It was called the Jerusalem Virus and it **deleted** files every Friday the 13th. This day is believed to be unlucky in any month. It was unlucky for those who lost important files.

In 1991 a virus called Michelangelo hit the **network.** It ruined many **hard drives** on March 6, the birthday of the painter Michelangelo.

The **FBI** website has been attacked by hackers.

Would you believe it?

In 1999 a hacker group called phreak.nl damaged U.S. **websites.** The vandals spread the message "**Hack** the Planet." Another message appeared on the White House website. It said in large red letters: "Hacker wuz Here." Although this was the only damage done, it showed that even the best security systems could be broken.

David Smith being arrested for cyber crime in 1999.

chaos   total confusion

Famous names

Cyber vandals were very busy through the 1990s. So were the police.

1992	A teenager who wrote the Satan Bug Virus was arrested in Washington, D.C. He was too young to be named or to be sent to prison.
1994	Christopher Pile was the first person to go to prison in the United Kingdom for writing a virus. He was eighteen years old.
1996	A virus called Concept became the most common virus in the world.
1999	A virus called Melissa became the fastest virus ever. It caused $80 million in damage. David Smith from New Jersey admitted to writing it. He went to prison for five years.

Did you know?

- Around 200 viruses are at work at any given time.
- More than 60 new viruses appear every month.
- Nearly 65,000 viruses have gone around the Internet in the last twenty years. They have caused about $65 billion damage in the United States alone. Any computer is at risk. The police are
- now clamping down on this form of cyber crime.

hard drive   computer's main data-storage device that runs the hard disk

21st century vandals

The new **millennium** brought new cyber **vandals.** The **virus** known as the Love Bug arrived as an email in May 2000. Everyone wanted to open its message: "I love you." This was a big mistake. Love Bug spread so widely that it **infected** 1 in 28 of the world's emails!

Prison

In 2003, 22-year-old Simon Vallor of the United Kingdom went to prison for two years. He pleaded guilty to writing and sending out three computer viruses. These were called Gokar, Redesi, and Admirer. They infected about 27,000 computers in 42 countries.

Virus causes billions in damage

The I LOVE YOU virus often comes from someone known to the user. It spreads automatically from their computer's address book. The virus destroys files and searches for names and passwords. These are sent back to a secret email address. So far no one has been **convicted** for creating and releasing this virus. The total damage has cost almost $10 billion.

Re:

Email Virus: Do NOT open emails with "i love you" in the s...

unknown

Fwd: Chinese tradition!! (xx)

Re: Labutis

Saff Memo 04/27/00

Word Bank   bandit   robber or outlaw who belongs to a gang

Warning—2001

A powerful new Windows computer virus is causing **chaos** with emails across the world. Experts say the Goner virus is spreading fast. They are warning computer users to **delete** it. It was first **detected** in the United States, but experts believe it was created in Europe.

The United States, the United Kingdom, France, and Australia are the worst hit of the seventeen countries affected so far. Goner can even disable **anti-virus software** in a computer. The email is simply named "hi" and arrives with an attachment.

Size

How are you? When I saw this screensaver I immediately thought of you. I promise you'll love it.

Do not open this attachment!

Who wrote the Goner virus?

Five Israeli teenagers, one still in middle school, were charged at the end of 2001. "They are not **bandits,** they are regular kids," said the head of the Israeli police computer crimes squad. "They are not computer experts, although one of them could write a **program.** I don't think they fully understood what they were doing."

05/04/00

05/04/00

05/02/00

04/30/00

04/30/00

04/24/00

Despite the warning, thousands of people opened the Love Bug.

Cyber cafés are getting more and more popular.

detect   discover a crime

The year of the worm

2003 was the year of the **worm.** It was also the year of catching the worm makers.

But no one knows who made the Slammer worm. Also known as the Sapphire worm, Slammer hit the **Internet** on January 25, 2003. It was the fastest-moving cyber attack yet. The number of hits doubled every 8.5 seconds. Slammer did 90 percent of its damage in the first ten minutes of its release.

The worm **crashed** parts of the Internet in South Korea and Japan. It disrupted the phone service in Finland and slowed down airline booking systems, **credit card networks,** and bank machines in the United States.

Big worms

In 2003 the Sobig worms began to strike. Sobig F was the sixth version of the worm that infected email **programs.** It flooded **servers** and used infected computers to spread itself further. The system could not cope with all the email traffic. One **anti-virus** company said Sobig F was one of the fastest-spreading worms ever.

Names like Slammer or Blaster describe how fast and furious worms spread outward. They "explode" across the Internet.

genius   someone with amazing ability and intelligence

Blaster

The Blaster worm was also released in 2003. But there was not just one worm, and each type was slightly different. The worms **infected** one in five companies around the world. Help-lines to computer companies became clogged, and many businesses had to close. Blaster stopped personal computers from connecting to the Internet.

People were arrested. Each worked alone. In Romania a 24-year-old man was charged with sending out Blaster F. He said it was an accident, but such crimes still carry a fifteen-year prison sentence. An American teenager was arrested for creating the Blaster B worm. The **FBI** had been watching him for some time.

August 29, 2003

US TEENAGER HELD OVER EMAIL WORM

An eighteen-year-old high school student from Minnesota has been charged with creating a Blaster worm. He faces up to ten years in prison and a fine of $250,000. A neighbor said he was "a computer **genius**" but not a criminal. His version of the worm infected around 7,000 computers.

Cyber Theft

Hackers: the movie

In this 1995 movie (below), the **FBI** arrest a boy for writing a computer **virus**. He is banned from using a computer until his eighteenth birthday. Years later, he and his friends uncover a plot by a cyber vandal to release a nasty computer virus. They must find evidence to convince the FBI, while keeping ahead of the criminal.

Cyber **vandals** do not get rich. Cyber thieves might, if they hit the right bank. Some thieves simply **hack** into a bank to transfer money to their account. Then they withdraw the stolen money.

Other cyber thieves hack into a bank's security files and find account numbers, passwords, and **PINs.** If they can steal someone's bank card, they can get cash from any bank at any time. But few people get away with such crimes. Banks notice the movement of money and will soon call the police.

In the James Bond movie *Golden Eye*, Alan Cumming plays a computer programmer/hacker.

Word Bank   PIN   Personal Identification Number; code used to get into a bank account

Spying

How useful it would be to get access to the secrets of a **rival** company! If you knew all its plans, you could figure out how to beat it. If you could break into their computer records to change a few figures, who would know? Hacking into rival computer files has been going on for years. Even "just looking" is a form of spying. It is called theft of ideas.

Hacking into a country's defense system to find out its **military** secrets is cyber spying. Changing a few codes to disable an enemy's missiles or to fire them may not happen only in James Bond movies! Today, companies' computer systems can soon **detect** hackers at work.

Mission impossible?

The FBI and **CSI** held a survey of U.S. businesses in 2002. Half of the companies said cyber spying by competitors was a big concern. Thirty-six percent had experienced electronic break-ins during the past year.

> " Rival companies are the single greatest threat in computer crime. "

Richard Power of the CSI, 2003

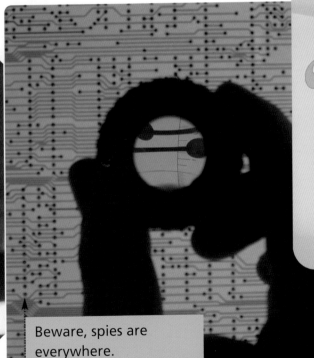

Beware, spies are everywhere.

Daylight robbery

Online banking makes life much easier for people and businesses. But it also makes a thief's life easier. Computers have opened up a world of big-time **fraud.**

Breaking into computer systems to sell information to criminal groups can make large amounts of money. A hacker just needs to get hold of someone's **credit card** details. To do this, some cyber criminals pretend to be the bank and email a message. They ask the victim to log on to a **website** to confirm card numbers and passwords.

Of course, the website is a **fake,** but it looks just like the bank's real one. Anyone who is fooled gives away important details.

Bank robbers can now work from home!

illegal   against the law

Bedroom thief

Even small-time crooks can get into big-time cyber theft. In 2000 a teenager from the United Kingdom used his computer to find the details of 25,000 credit cards. He posted the details to a website for anyone else to use. In the United States, the **FBI** was soon on to him. The U.K. police then caught him.

> Mr. Gray, eighteen, was arrested in Wales after an FBI investigation into credit card fraud. He now faces ten charges of **downloading illegal** information, under the Computer Misuse Act of 1990.

Gray pleaded guilty to theft and **hacking,** but he said he had not made any money from this. He was sentenced to three years of community service, or working to help people in the area for no pay.

Australian theft

In a 2003 survey, 47 percent of Australian companies said they had suffered from cyber crime over the last two years.

That was more than North America (41 percent) and Western Europe (34 percent). Almost half of these Australian companies were never able to get their money back.

The business center of Sydney, Australia, is under attack from cyber crime.

fake   false, not real

More than a game

Computer games are a multimillion dollar business. Fans eagerly wait for each new game to come out. Favorite characters and special effects get better all the time. That is, unless thieves get there first.

Fans of the game Half-Life waited for Half-Life 2 to come out in October 2003. But it all went wrong. A hacker broke into Valve, the company that makes the game. The thief stole Half-Life 2's **source code**. A **pirate copy** of the new game was then released on the **Internet.** Valve had to stop the game from being sold, losing huge amounts of money. Fans had to wait for the real game to come out in 2004.

Cyber criminals steal someone else's identity in order to steal their money or buy things with their bank cards.

pirate copy   version of a CD, DVD, or game that has been copied illegally

Copyright

If you write a song or a story, you hope no one copies it and says it belongs to them. After all, they might get paid for it. The law of **copyright** is supposed to protect your work from being used without your permission.

But computers have made breaking copyright laws easy. It is simple to copy all kinds of material with a computer. If your best friend wanted to borrow some **software,** would you lend any of yours? They could then copy it and load it onto their computer without buying it. But copying **programs** and games is **illegal.** Would you still do it?

Copy crime

Copying from the Internet can get you into trouble. Many students have **downloaded** essays and passed them off as their own. This is called **plagiarism.** It is a form of theft and it is illegal.

Downloading information is completely legal on Apple's new online music store.

Cyber Terrorism

An expert says . . .

"There are a lot of different people who could conduct cyber warfare. There are criminal groups engaging in cyber crime. There are also some terrorist groups looking at using cyber attack."

Richard Clarke,
U.S. Adviser for
Cyberspace
Security, 2003

We have all come to depend on computers. They run our banks, workplaces, transportation, power grids, defense, health, police, and fire services. If all the computer **networks** failed, civilization would grind to a halt. If all **hard drives** were wiped clean, the world would plunge into **chaos.** Panic would rule. All **data** would be lost.

Such a nightmare may well be the dream of a criminal in a James Bond movie. Some of today's terrorists would take great pleasure in closing down the world's computers. Could they ever do it? Perhaps it is just a matter of time.

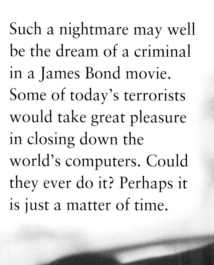

The army responds to cyber attacks as well as **military** crises on the ground.

Word Bank   **virus**   small piece of software that attaches to a computer program and harms it

Risk of terrorism

Cyber **terrorism** is the use of computers to scare or harm people. With just a hard drive, **modem,** and keyboard, terrorists could control **stock markets.** They could alter government security codes or even take over the world's weapons. Is this just **science fiction**?

Because the **Internet** has no boundaries, an organization such as al-Qaeda, which was responsible for the September 11, 2001, attacks, could break into computers from anywhere. It might get hold of top secret information. It could spread messages to scare people. Many governments now take the risk of cyber terrorism very seriously.

U.S. law

In 2003 tough new punishments came in for certain types of cyber crime. A **virus** sender who intends to cause death by jamming emergency telephone lines could now face life in prison. It may only be a matter of time before someone puts this to the test.

In *The Truman Show,* a powerful computer network is used to create a fantasy world.

modem   electronic device used to connect computers by a telephone line
stock market   buying and selling of stocks and shares

Threats

Threats made to scare people are a form of **terrorism.** Threats warning a bank that its computer files will be destroyed are a form of cyber terrorism. Terrorists may use **blackmail**: "If you don't pay up, we will destroy your **data** and tell the world." Banks might prefer to pay money rather than let people know how **vulnerable** they are. This kind of terrorism has happened, before bank computers had modern security.

From 1993 to 1995, banks in the United States and United Kingdom paid out around $735 million to cyber terrorists. Some only paid after computers were made to **crash.**

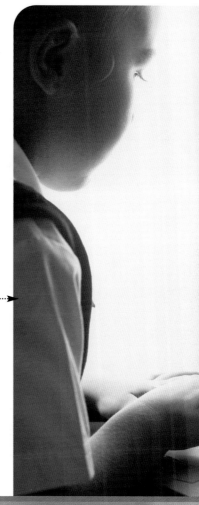

All computers are possible targets of cyber crime.

A minor threat?

" When I think about the various threats we face, I think that dangers such as nuclear weapons (below) will do much more harm than a cyber attack. Having said that, we have to take the cyber threat seriously, too. "

Scott Charney,
Chief Security,
Microsoft, 2002

blackmail   use of threats to get money from a victim

Do not panic

Billions of dollars are being spent on fighting the terror threat. The **FBI** has 1,000 "cyber investigators" on the lookout. They have yet to spot a real threat.

Will terrorists swap bombs and bullets for a mouse and **modem**? This is unlikely. Explosions and deaths will always get more attention than cyber attacks. Many security experts think that too much fuss is made about cyber threats. After all, the top-secret **military** computers are not even linked to the **World Wide Web.** No one "out there" can ever **hack** into them. Even so, the computer world will always have to stay on its guard.

What if . . .

Some people fear the worst. What if terrorists break into computers across the world? Could they close down all our power stations? Would the world be left in darkness? What if they break into hospital records? Could patients be given deadly doses of drugs? This is the stuff of **science fiction**. We hope!

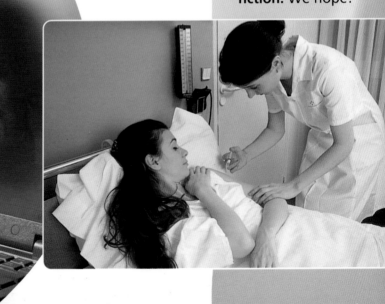

vulnerable   easily harmed or damaged

Big companies and banks were once the main target of cyber crime. Not any more. Anyone with a computer who goes on the **Internet** is at risk. But how can you tell if you are a victim? There may be some telltale signs. Has your computer **crashed online**? Has **software** suddenly stopped working correctly? Has a file disappeared for no reason? These could be signs that you are under attack.

If you start getting a lot of **spam** emails, you may ask how they all find you. If you find money has disappeared from your bank account, that could be the final proof. It is time to fight back!

Police seize computers of suspected cyber criminals.

Keeping ahead

If your computer slows down on the Internet, keep watch. If you cannot connect to **websites,** hang up and redial. A hacker might be **downloading** files from your computer. Someone out there could be breaking into your system. It may be time to protect your computer with new software.

Police are getting better at catching cyber criminals.

deter   prevent someone from doing a particular thing

The battle

Cyber crime will not go away. It is a growing problem. The challenge is to deal with it and stop it from disrupting people's work. It costs countries a fortune and can even be a danger to people's lives. By making cyber crime harder to carry out and easier to **detect,** computer experts hope to make it tougher for criminals. The aim is to prevent crimes from happening in the first place.

Punishment

Police across the world are working hard to **deter** cyber criminals. Their message is clear:
- the police are getting better at catching cyber criminals;
- the law is getting tougher on those who get caught.

Getting tough

From November 2003, judges in the United States began handing out tougher sentences. Hackers whose crimes result in injury or death now face from twenty years to life in prison. Sentences have now increased by 50 percent for hackers who share stolen personal **data** with anyone else.

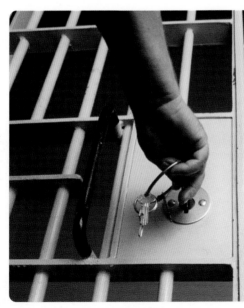

Keep out!

About 300 million computer users are now connected to each other on the **World Wide Web.** But security has tended to lag behind in the rush to get everyone **online.** Each link to the **network** is an open door to a criminal. "Locks" and new ways to keep them out are being developed all the time.

Keeping alert

The great thing about the **Internet** is that it lets people around the world share information and ideas quickly. But such freedom is open to **abuse.** Stricter rules and controls are always being made to keep one step ahead of the criminals.

Fitting better locks and alarms on a house will make it more **secure** against thieves. In the same way, it is wise to fit the latest "locks" to computers. Updating **anti-virus software** is one way to keep ahead of cyber **vandals.** Another is to fit software called a **firewall.** This is like a guard to keep out emails and **data** that could harm a computer.

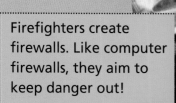

Firefighters create firewalls. Like computer firewalls, they aim to keep danger out!

36
Word Bank firewall   software to stop certain messages from getting into computers from the Internet

One step ahead

Firefighters often burn areas ahead of an advancing fire to stop flames from getting through. In the same way, a computer firewall is meant to keep danger out. It should "burn up" any incoming "bombs." If a cyber vandal tries to send you an email bomb, a firewall should keep it from getting into your inbox.

An email bomb is when someone sends you the same email hundreds or thousands of times until your email system **crashes.**

Even though good **software** tries to keep out criminals, it might never be 100 percent crimeproof. After all, hackers are always at work, ready to crack their next challenge.

Crimeproof?

Security software is like a traffic cop watching cars flow past your gate. It checks each one that slows down or looks like a suspect. But it might not notice the bike squeezing through the hedge in the backyard!

Following the Rules

Following the Rules

On a recent poster

" Would you go into a store and steal a CD? It's the same thing when people log on to computers and steal our music. "

Britney Spears (below)

How easy is it to become a cyber criminal? Many people do not realize they may be doing something **illegal** on their computer. Even trying to guess another person's password is wrong. After all, it is "entering a computer without permission," which is against the law.

Breaking into someone's email account is also illegal. You need to be careful when using chat rooms and sending emails. Using words or pictures that are racist or **obscene** may be breaking the law. If you **download** or pass on material that others find annoying, untrue, or **offensive,** you could also be committing a crime.

Word Bank

culprit   someone guilty of a crime
defense   case to support what you have done

Stealing from artists

Many people download videos or music on the **Internet.** Record companies may let you copy some free samples. Otherwise, it is illegal to copy music. Yet over 2.6 billion music files are downloaded without permission every month.

An MP3 file is a special way of sending music tracks over the Internet. But this has led to music piracy, which is when people swap music instead of buying the CD. It means bands do not sell their music and their work is being stolen. The music industry loses about $4 billion each year in this way.

If you try to get the latest hits free online, you might be breaking the law.

obscene   indecent material that offends people
offensive   shocking, upsetting, or insulting

Staying safe

So how can ordinary computer users protect themselves from cyber criminals? Although there may only be a few of them out there, it pays to keep up your guard. After all, no one would leave a new car with its doors open and keys in the ignition. Computers, too, need some security and common sense to stop criminals from **abusing** them.

Remember:
- Never give people your password and always log off after you have finished on a **website.**
- Be careful when using chat rooms. People you chat with are not always who they say they are.
- Never give your address or phone number to anyone you meet on the **Internet.**

It is important to keep your computer **secure.** You would not leave the doors open on a brand new sports car!

CIA   Central Intelligence Agency of the United States
corporation   large organization or company

More advice

- Never arrange to meet someone you chat with on the Internet.
- If you buy anything **online,** make sure you have full details of the company you are buying from. Keep records of your order and number, in case something goes wrong.
- Never open an email attachment unless you are sure what it is. It is easy to release a **worm** just by opening it. If in doubt, **delete** it right away.
- If you get an email warning of a **virus** telling you to send this warning to everyone in your address book, do not do it! These are usually **hoaxes.** If in doubt, you can check with an Internet security firm.

What they say . . .

"

It's power at your fingertips. You can control all these computers from the government, from the **military,** from large **corporations.** And if you know what you're doing, you can travel through the Internet at your will, with no **restrictions.** That's power.

"

A cyber criminal who broke into **NASA's** computers and later went to prison, 2001

restriction rule to stop you from doing something

Living proof

Soon you may have to give more than just a password to use a computer. After all, how does the computer know you are not a **fake**? Before long, machines may need to read your fingerprint (below) before they let you log on. All you will need to do is press your finger against the screen.

What next?

Just 50 years ago, no one could ever have imagined today's cyber world. In another 50 years, who knows how it will have changed? Will cyber crime be a thing of the past? Probably not.

The **Internet** seems to attract people who like to disturb others. From **vandals,** spies, or thieves to people who keep sending annoying emails. There are also criminal groups that communicate with others across the world to plot their crimes on the Internet. They include drug dealers, **software** thieves, and people with extreme political views who want to encourage hatred of others. Such crimes are always out there.

Your eye, like your fingerprint, is unique. Reading your eye will tell a computer if it is really you.

Word Bank   recognize   identify who someone is

Future possibilities

Computers may soon **recognize** voices. Or they will study eyes. By reading your **retina,** the computer will know if it is really you. Only then will it let you log on.

The Internet continues to be a great learning tool, since it opens up new worlds and new ideas. The more people communicate, the more they understand each other. That can only be a good thing. But there is still a tiny fraction of computer users who only see possibilities for greed, mischief, or even terror. The cyber world, just like the real world, will sadly never be totally free of crime and the fear it brings.

retina   area at the back of the eyeball

Security

Two-thirds of U.K. companies have experienced a serious security incident such as **hacking, virus** attacks, or **credit card fraud** in the past year.

Hackers are seen as the main threat to cyber security. Former employees and organized crime have also been blamed for some of this crime.

If you want to find out more about the criminal underworld, take a look at these books:

Knittel, John et al. *Everything You Need to Know About the Dangers of Coputer Hacking.* New York: Rosen, 2000.

McIntosh, Neil. *Face the Facts: Cyber Crime.* Chicago: Raintree, 2003.

Woolf, Alex. *Forensic Files: Investigating Thefts and Heists.* Chicago: Heinemann, 2004.

Did you know?

In Australia it is a crime in some states to:

- own a mattress without a mattress license;
- wear pink short-shorts after midday on Sundays;
- change a lightbulb unless you are an electrician!

Criminal records

- The world's first speeding ticket was issued in the United Kingdom in 1896 to a man named Walter Arnold. He was traveling at 8 mph (13 km/h) in a 2 mph (3.25 km/h) zone.

- The most successful sniffer dog was a Labrador from the United States named Snag. He found 118 different hoards of hidden drugs worth an amazing $1 billion!

- The oldest person to be hanged was 82-year-old Allan Mair in 1843 in the U.K. He was hanged sitting down, since he was unable to stand.

- The world's largest safety-deposit-box robbery took place in 1976. A group of highly trained criminals stole more than $39 million worth of goods from a bank in the Middle East.

Robbery

Cyber criminals robbed Americans of more than $437 million in 2003. The most common ways include: using stolen identities, **fake Internet** auctions, and shop-at-home pages. You have been warned!

Glossary

abuse wrongful use

accessing getting inside

anti-virus software software that tracks down a computer virus and makes it safe

bandit robber or outlaw who belongs to a gang

blackmail use of threats to get money from a victim

boot sector program that loads a computer's operating system

chaos total confusion

CIA Central Intelligence Agency of the United States

convicted found guilty of committing a crime

copyright law that protects someone's work from being copied by others

corporation large organization or company

crash shut down suddenly

credit card plastic card used to buy goods right away; the bill is paid later

CSI Computer Security Institute of the United States

culprit someone guilty of a crime

data information stored on computers

defense case to support what you have done

delete remove

detect discover

deter prevent someone from doing a particular thing

download put information from the Internet onto your computer

fake false, not real

FBI Federal Bureau of Investigation, which deals with serious crime in the United States

firewall software to stop certain messages from getting into computers from the Internet

fraud false or dishonest trick to get money

genius someone with amazing ability and intelligence

hack gain access to a computer illegally

hard disk main storage space and memory on a computer

hard drive computer's main data-storage device that runs the hard disk

hoax practical joke

icon image or sign on a computer screen

illegal against the law

infect pass on something harmful to someone else

Internet worldwide network that links smaller computer networks together

Microsoft company that made and runs Windows and other major programs

military armed forces of a country

millennium period of one thousand years

modem electronic device used to connect computers by a telephone line

NASA National Aeronautics and Space Administration; the U.S. space organization

network system of computers connected by communication lines

obscene indecent material that shocks or upsets people

offensive shocking, upsetting, or insulting

online when a computer is linked up "live" to the Internet

penalty punishment for breaking the law

PIN Personal Identification Number; code used to get into a bank account

pirate copy version of a CD, DVD, or game that has been copied illegally

plagiarism copying someone else's writing or ideas and pretending they are your own

probation time of supervision instead of prison, when behavior must be good

program series of instructions that tell a computer how to do something

recognize identify who someone is

restriction rule to stop you from doing something

retina area at the back of the eyeball

rival person or team competing against another person or team

science fiction made-up stories that may twist the facts of science

secure safe against attack

server central machine that runs a network of computers

software systems that run computers and allow them to do different tasks

source code "engine" that runs a computer game

spam electronic "junk mail"

stand alone computer that is not linked up to any other computer

stock market buying and selling of stocks and shares

terrorism trying to scare or hurt people

vandal person who sets out to destroy or damage someone else's property

vandalism destroying or damaging the property of others

virus small piece of software that attaches to a computer program and harms it

vulnerable easily harmed or damaged

website set of pages of information on the Internet about a particular subject

World Wide Web part of the Internet that is easy to search for information

worm small piece of software that enters computers and makes copies of itself